POSITIVE THINKING

CHANGE YOUR ATTITUDE, CHANGE YOUR LIFE!

OPTIMISM, MINDSET, SELF IMPROVEMENT & BRAIN TRAINING

THEO GOLD

© 2015

COPYRIGHT NOTICE

All rights reserved.

No part of this publication may be reproduced, distributed, or transmitted in any form or by any means; including, photocopying, recording, or other electronic or mechanical methods, without the prior written permission of the publisher, except in the case of brief quotations embodied in critical reviews and certain other non-commercial uses permitted by copyright law.

DISCLAIMER

Although the author and publisher have made every effort to ensure that the information in this book was correct at press time, the author and publisher do not assume and hereby disclaim any liability to any party for any loss, damage, or disruption caused by errors or omissions, whether such errors or omissions result from negligence, accident, or any other cause.

Table of Contents

COPYRIGHT NOTICE ii

DISCLAIMER iii

INTRODUCTION 1

THE POWER OF NEGATIVE THINKING 7

TAKING THE FIRST STEP 11

TAKING THE FIRST STEP 14

FOCUSING ON WHERE YOU ARE 18

BECOMING SELF-AWARE 25

OVERCOMING NEGATIVITY IN OTHERS 33

OVERCOMING PROCRASTINATION 38

NO TIME LIKE THE PRESENT 42

INTRODUCTION

You have the power within yourself to succeed at just about anything you put your mind to. I know this statement may seem far-fetched to you, as it is to most people who first hear it, but the truth is that the only thing that is holding you back from achieving the level of success you have only dreamed about is your own mind. Your brain is your most powerful tool, and believe it or not, you can train your brain to succeed or you can train your brain to fail. The problem is that the majority of the time, we are training our brain to fail, time after time.

Many of us do this day after day, until it becomes almost automatic. We usually are quite unaware of our thinking patterns and wonder why nothing ever seems to work out for us. We don't realize that our very patterns of thought are what is causing our failure. When we tell ourselves over and over that we cannot succeed, we find that time and time again we are unable to succeed which tends to reinforce our own belief that we are not able to succeed, until it becomes a pattern of negativity that we seem unable to break.

This book is about breaking that pattern of negativity by changing the way you think and thereby changing your life. Wouldn't it be nice to be confident in the knowledge that everything you set your mind to will actually work out for you? Wouldn't it be nice to realize that you are in control of life's circumstances instead of constantly being knocked back by life's circumstances? Wouldn't it be nice, for a change, to be the one in the driver's seat? Well, guess what? You can be that person in control of life, you can be the pilot of your destiny. You don't have to sit back and watch as life pushes you around, taking you away from your goals and shattering you hopes and dreams.

There are many out there who will read this introduction and believe that it's written for someone else, or that it is just not true. They believe that there is almost nothing they can do about unforeseen circumstances that cause them to fail in their endeavors. There are way too many people who will read this and say "Life doesn't work that way.". They are drawing on their past (or present) experiences and saying to themselves that circumstances "beyond their control" have led them to this conclusion that they have no control over their own life. They truly believe this to be the case, because they have proven it to themselves over and over again.

For example, that man living in poverty was born into poverty, his parents were poor, his grandparents were poor, and he is poor, he has no education as he can't afford to go to college, he is living off of the system, because he has no skills and/or cannot find a job. He says to himself, "this is just the way it is, it's always been this way, and it will always be this way" and he just continues the pattern of poverty.

He truly believes that he is meant to live in poverty. He may dream of someday striking it rich, of winning the lottery or maybe finding a valuable treasure buried somewhere. But it's only a dream to him. One that he knows won't come true. He is born into poverty and he knows in his heart he will die in poverty. That's just the way it is and nothing will ever change.

This may seem an extreme example to many, but it is happening all over this country and all over the world today. This is a mindset, albeit an extreme mindset, that many people are actually living with every day, believing themselves to be "doomed" to a life of poverty. It becomes their reality that this is the way it is, and as much as they would like for it to change, they know it won't. They believe that they are destined to be destitute and no amount of "wishful thinking" is going to change their circumstances.

Now, you may not be living in abject poverty, but you probably aren't living the life you really want to live, or you wouldn't be reading this book. You might have enough money to get by, but are constantly battling your debt, credit card bills, mortgage payments, etc. You may have gotten to the point that you have come to accept that this is just the way it's meant to be, that you will never be free from your debt, possibly that you aren't meant to be. Maybe you have tried to live according to a budget, cutting your spending on "frivolous" items, refusing to go out to eat, etc. But yet, it seems no matter how much you try, something always comes up and it puts you right back under that ocean of debt. You find yourself just treading water, trying to keep your head up, but finding yourself drowning in a sea of bills.

This situation is also, unfortunately, happening all over the world as well. Financial gurus will tell you that these people are "living beyond their means", which is just a fancy way of saying they are getting what they want, what they deserve, but it's costing them more than they can afford. If all of your bills equal more than your actual income, then you are living beyond your means. The only viable solution they can find, if they don't want to end up in poverty, is to cut their expenses. Maybe they sell their house, cut their groceries to just the necessities, stop going out to eat, etc. Until they are able to get on top of their mountain of debt, which might take the rest of their lives. In other words, they deprive themselves of the good things in life simply to make ends meet.

Often, the above solution is the only one that people can see. Any other solution is wishful thinking. They aren't going to inherit a million dollars, they won't win the lottery, and doubtful they will get a better job that makes them more money. So they end up going through life, just getting by. Someday, they may have actually climbed out of debt (or they may never) but in doing so, they have also lived a miserly life, devoid of any happiness or contentment. Never able to do what they really want to do, go where they want to go or even be who they wish they could be.

What if I could tell you there is another solution to this problem. That you don't have to deprive yourself of those things that make life worth living in order to live your life. What if I told you held within your own mind the ability to change your circumstances without having to go without, on the contrary, what if you could overcome your debt while having everything you desire? Seem like a pipe dream? Well it's not impossible, and many people are doing just that today. They have learned the secret of overcoming a life of deprivation and despair and coming out on top. The secret that they have discovered is simple, yet profound.

That secret is what this book is about, and it's such a simple thing that many people simply discount it because they believe it is too good to be true. They believe in the old adage that "if it seems too good to be true, it probably is" and therefore discount it out of hand, never even taking the time to actually verify whether or not it is true. Instead of being disappointed by another failure, they choose to live where they are and hope for the best, expecting the worse.

Perhaps that's where you are at right now? Instead of taking a leap of faith and risk falling on your face, you have decided you will keep your feet firmly on the ground and just accept that this is what life is, there is no more and you have no control over your circumstances. Obviously, however, you have picked up this book for a reason. Maybe it was just curiosity or maybe you believe there may be a glimmer of hope, maybe there is a way you can change your life. Just possibly, you are reading this book because you believe that the "status quo" is a lie and you really do have it in you to change. I hope you are this latter person, because this book is written for you. If you don't believe there is any hope, than I'm sorry to say, this book may actually not be able to help you.

It's not that the principles outlined in this book are not true. The problem is that you must at least open your mind to the possibility that there is hope, that you can really change and that you can be better off than you are. Even if you are not that person drowning under debt, or that person living in abject poverty, you may still feel trapped within your life, unable to move forward, unable to succeed in realizing your dreams or making you goals. Regardless of where you are, you must believe that there is a better way. Even if it's only a begrudging nod toward the slight possibility that there might be something in this Positive Thinking thing, that's at least a mustard seed of faith, and that is all you really need, a willingness to give this a chance, to step out on that limb and take a leap of faith, even if you are fearful at first of falling on your face. Once you realize that the principles within this guidebook are solid principles, you will find that not only were your fears unfounded but that they were actually part of the problem. Once you have started living according to these principles you will find that it's not so much about "wishful thinking" as it about "right thinking" and you will realize, by changing your mind and changing your attitude you have always had it in your power to change your life.

THE POWER OF NEGATIVE THINKING

The title of this chapter may not be what you were expecting, as most books on positive thinking are focused on the power of positive thinking, but it's important to realize the flip side of the same coin. There is quite a bit of power in negative thinking as well, and by realizing this we may understand much better why positive thinking works as it does.

When we focus on the negative in life, we tend to draw negative from life. For instance, when we consider our circumstances and continually tell ourselves how miserable we are, how we can't seem to get ahead, how life is just full of disappointments, we draw on the negative powers and actually attract more negativity in our life. It's a vicious cycle that we put ourselves in, we focus on the negative, draw to ourselves more negative, focus more on that negative, and on and on, until our lives seem to be nothing but negative outcomes.

So the first thing we need to do is realize how much power Negative Thinking has over our life, before we can break the bonds that bind us to our own failures. When we think "we can't" we are setting ourselves up for failure. Every thought and statement we make goes to our brain, where our subconscious minds attempt to make it reality. So, if I say "I can't get out of debt" what my brain is doing is sending an message to my subconscious mind telling it "You cannot get out of debt, make this a reality" so my subconscious mind goes about creating circumstances to make my "wish" it's command, like a genie in a bottle.

I might, in reality, really want the opposite to be true, but that's not what my brain is picking up on, what my brain is hearing is "I cannot" and it works on that presumption. If I really want to get out of debt, the worse thing I can think or say is that I cannot do it. Unfortunately, this is often the exact thing we do when faced with a negative situation, we dwell on that negativity telling ourselves "i can't get ahead" or "I'm unable to find that job I want" or "I don't know how to be happy" or a myriad of other cant's won'ts and don'ts... we feed ourselves on negative thoughts and then sit back and wonder why so much of our life is in turmoil.

Our subconscious mind is much like a computer we are programming with every thought and statement we make. The program doesn't "know" anything, it cannot "reason" our intent, it just picks up on what we program it. If we make a statement such as "this will never work out", our subconscious mind adds this to the program, telling our conscious mind (on a subconscious level) to make it so that "this will never work out" because that is what the programmer (you) says is real. This will also work with statements such as "why can't things ever go right". The subconscious will pick up on the part about things not going right, and ignore the "why" as its job is not to answer questions but to respond to the programmer's view of reality, to make it real (to realize it).

Once you understand this concept of how the mind works, you may begin to understand why the negative circumstances in your life seem to keep piling up. You keep realizing negative things and the mind keep making them into reality. I use the word realize here in the original sense of the word; to make real. When you tell yourself "I can't", your mind automatically goes to work making that concept real, it becomes reality. If a racer starts a race by thinking "I can't win this race", the odds are they will not win. If a person goes to get a job and thinks "they won't hire me", there is a good chance they won't be hired. It's just the way the mind works, it puts into action the thoughts it is fed. It does everything it can to make your thoughts and statements into reality, regardless of the detrimental nature of the thoughts.

Once you understand this very basic concept of how your subconscious mind works, then you can begin to see how you have been programming your mind to failure. It's not that you want to fail, but that you tell yourself that this is what is real. You might as well be saying "I am a failure", when you ask yourself "Why can't I be successful" as your subconscious mind will take both to mean the same thing and will react accordingly. Tell your mind "you are a failure" and you will fail again and again.

This "conditioning" has been probably going on for a long, long time. It may not be as drastic as you being a complete failure in everything you do, but as long as you have been saying "I can't do this" or "I can't do that" or "why can't I do this", you have been programming (or conditioning) your mind to accept that you don't have the ability to do that thing you want to do, regardless of what that thing is. It's become ingrained in your mind, over and over, as you have possibly attempted to succeed and have seen yourself fail. Each time you have failed, you probably have said to yourself "See... I am a failure... I can't ever succeed" and of course you don't, won't and can't succeed.

So, you see the power that negative thinking has over your life. You are at the mercy of those negative thoughts, seemingly in an endless cycle. Even if you try to say "I am a success" you will probably not believe it. It's not the reality you have made, it's not the situation you have programmed your mind to realize, and it's simply not real to you that you are a success. So you may be wondering, however can I break out of this cycle of negativity that I have trapped myself in? Can I ever be free from my negativity?

The answer is, YES you can! But don't expect to be an overnight success, and don't expect it to be an easy journey. You have been conditioning yourself (as well as being conditioned by others) for years and years, and it's not something you simply undo by some magical incantation. There is no easy road to successfully ridding yourself of negativity, but the good news is, you CAN be free from this negative bondage, and you CAN start changing your can'ts into can's. It will take time, but with effort and determination, you can and will be free of that powerful enemy of your mind; that power of negative thinking.

TAKING THE FIRST STEP

As we learned in the previous chapter, the impact of negative thoughts and affirmations has conditioned your mind to believe that you cannot do that which you want to do. You have, in essence, taught yourself that this is reality, that you are unable to be who you want to be, do what you want to do, achieve what you want to achieve, etc. and you are stuck in this rut. You want to change, but you are so ingrained in believing you cannot, that your own mind tells you that you can't change.

I imagine that the reason you purchased or borrowed this book is because you realize that there is something wrong and you really want to change your life. I think it's safe to say that you are tired of always wanting but never having that life you dare to dream is possible and you are just looking for an answer. However, I'll also bet there is that voice in the back of your mind saying, this isn't going to help, this isn't going to work, you can't succeed in this, this is just a pipe dream, this book isn't going to help you at all. Do you hear that voice? If so, then the first step you need to take is in learning how to silence that little voice that is constantly telling you that you can't, and this chapter is about showing you how to take that first step.

The first thing you must realize is that YOU have created that voice and you can control that voice. You can silence that voice by negating the negative with a positive. Try it now. Say in a loud and firm voice, "I am changing now!" Don't say "I am going to change" or even "I can change" but say "I am changing". When you put your affirmation in the present tense, as something that is happening NOW, then your mind will be much more receptive to this affirmation. Of course, depending on how much negative programming (or conditioning) you have created in your mind, a simple affirmation such as this one probably won't automatically affect that change in you, at least not immediately.

You must not only say you are changing, you must believe you are changing. Of course, if you stop and think about it, you ARE changing, every day, every second of every minute of every day you are changing, you are different now than you were two paragraphs ago. You have new thoughts, new ideas, new insights you may not have had before, you are not the same person you once were, and you will not be the same person you are now 10 minutes in the future. But the thing you must do is realize (there's that word again) that you are changing for the better. You are becoming a positive minded person.

By actually realizing this in your mind, you have taken a step toward training your brain to be positive. If you are becoming more positive, than you will continue to become more positive. You must continue to reaffirm this to yourself, telling yourself "I am becoming more positive now!". Keep your affirmation positive and try not to dwell on the negative. Don't say "I am not going to be negative", even if this sounds like the same thing. You see, when you say "not" and "negative" these can be picked up by your brain as "negative" thoughts, which it turns into negative reality. So even when the negatives are pointing toward the positive, it's still causing your brain to react negatively.

So, the very first step is affirming that you have taken this step. That, starting now (not tomorrow, not next week) you are changing, you are becoming more positive, you are growing and changing and being the person you know you can be. Believing it to be true (because it is true) and letting yourself accept this will start you on your way to a lifetime of positivity. Once you have ingrained in your mind that you are a positive person, your brain will be much more receptive to other positive thoughts and affirmations.

While you are convincing yourself that you are, in reality, becoming more positive, allow yourself to recognize that this book is helping you to become that positive person. Realize that this book is giving you the ability to see yourself as you really are and to take control of your mind (and therefore take control of your life) by getting rid of any negative thoughts that have hindered you in the past. The more positive minded you become the less power negative thoughts have over your mind, and vice versa. You have the power within yourself to effect this change and it all starts with the simple step of telling yourself that you are "changing your mind" and you are a positive minded person. From there it's only a matter of time until you start using that power of positive thinking in all aspects of your life.

TAKING THE FIRST STEP

There are probably a thousand books that have been written attempting to explain or explore the meaning of life. Most of us need meaning, we need to know that there is a reason we are here, a reason why we are even alive. Serious psychological depression sets in when we cannot find a meaning for our existence and unfortunately, many people take their own lives every year because of this.

The meaning of life is really quite simple, but profound. You create the meaning. There is no "meaning" to life, other than the meaning you give it. This may sound rather simplistic, and to some people it may even seem a preposterous notion. However, once you actually take this concept under serious consideration, you'll see that there cannot possibly be any other meaning to life, but the meaning you give it.

What you do with your life is the meaning you give to your life. If all you do is sit around watching t.v. all day, then that becomes the meaning of life for you. Not much of a meaning, to be sure, but the meaning of life is the meaning you give it.Some people feel there is no meaning, but that's because they have not given life a meaning, they have not decided to focus on what their life means to them and to live accordingly. Many people, especially the very young, have no objective in site, not goal in their life, no destination for their journey and often these people are the most depressed and the most negative minded people you will find.

Albert Einstein once quipped, "If you want to live a happy life, tie it to a goal, not to people or things." The problem is, however, too many people base their existential happiness on other people and things, having no personal goal in and of themselves. What happens when that person leaves them? Their "whole world crumbles". The same if they tie their happiness to possessions. When they lose those possessions, they have no basis for happiness, they find their world without meaning.

On the other hand, many people tie all of their happiness to that one main goal, and find themselves in a downward spiral when their goal is not being met. These people may, indeed, have a goal, but that goal is so high and so lofty that nothing else matter and they miss out on life completely, while they attempt to obtain that goal. When adverse circumstances come into the picture and they find they are not meeting their goal, they can become negative-minded, morose and depressed, as their world has no meaning, if the goal appears to become unattainable.

So what am I saying? We should or we should not have goals? Of course we should have goals, it is what makes us continue to reach and stretch, it gives us a meaning and a purpose, but our goals should not be what defines us. We should not let our goals be such that we are consumed by them. If we let our goals define our meaning of life, then our life will become meaningless until we actually obtain those goals and when something comes in the way of our realizing that goal, it might even seem like our whole world is falling apart.

So, while it's good to tie your happiness to a goal, to give your life more meaning, it's not good to become obsessed with that goal, or inflexible in obtaining the goal. As a matter of fact, it's good to have little goals that serve to get you closer to your main goal. For instance, if your goal is to become a great painter, you might have smaller goals, such as to take an art class, to paint your first picture, to sell your first painting, etc. Each smaller goal should get you closer to your main goal. These smaller goals are part of the meaning you are giving to your life, as well as your family and friends and other things that you feel make life worth living.

Some people might ask, "What if I have no goals, or any ambitions to speak of?" Which is a sad circumstance, because without any ambitions, we really are just moving through life with no direction and very little happiness. If you are one of those people who simply have not set goals and don't really seem to be going anywhere, just drifting through life, it's never too late to stop and take stock of your life. Ask yourself, if I could be anything, do anything in this world, what would it be? If you can answer that question, then that should be your goal. It doesn't matter how unattainable it might seem, and to be honest, there are some goals none of us will ever attain, but that shouldn't stop you from making the goals. Why? Because it's not the goal that is the thing, it is the journey.

This is why I say, don't allow yourself to become so consumed by your goal that it is the only important thing in your life. The real meaning of your life isn't the goal(s) you have set, it is the day to day journey toward obtaining those goals. It is the struggles, the adversity as well as the triumphs and victories! As you overcome obstacles, you find yourself growing and becoming stronger and more positive in your thinking and in your living. You cannot become stronger without resistance. That's an important lesson to remember. Body builders and most athletes already recognize this, that it takes resistance to build strength. This not only applies to muscular strength but to mental, psychological and emotional strength.

Many people think in order to have a meaningful life they should avoid any kind of struggle, but the opposite is true. Those who have not struggled for what they have are the ones who appreciate what they have the least. You can be a multi-billionaire and be able to get just about anything you want, but still be miserable. That's because it's not those possessions that help to give your life meaning, but rather it is your accomplishments toward gaining those possessions that give it meaning. Those people who always want everything for nothing are truly the most miserable people, because they have never known the joy in putting forth the effort toward obtaining their desires. They may never realize the struggles are what defines us, the trials and tribulations are what gives us character, these are what help in giving us meaning for our lives and our existence.

FOCUSING ON WHERE YOU ARE

Have you ever noticed that if you are driving a car (or a bicycle) and something grabs your attention on the side of the road, if you focus on that thing that grabbed your attention, you tend to navigate toward it? You often end up having to swerve the vehicle in order to avoid going off the road. Whatever it was that distracted us and made us change our focus causes us to subconsciously change our direction toward that object. It's usually not a conscious decision to go that way, it's just the way our brains are wired.

If we keep our focus on the road, we are fine, but when we lose our focus, we are in danger of losing the road. The same holds true of our goals. When we keep our mind on our goals, we tends to gravitate toward those goals, but when we take our minds off of that goal, getting distracted by some peripheral issue, we may find we are no longer moving toward that goal. It may be that we get so distracted that we completely lose site of the goal and by the time we realize it, we have gone "off the road".

When we have a goal, and we use our positive attitude to obtain that goal, we must remain focused on that goal, until such time as we have reached our destination (of getting what we want). This means we need to not allow things like other people, unexpected circumstances, tragic news stories, or other peripherals to allow us to change our focus and take our minds off of our goals.

Sometimes it's hard to keep that focus. For instance if something is in the news that we feel strongly for or against and we feel we must do something about it, we may end up focusing on taking care of that issue, possibly with the mindset of getting back on the road toward our goal at a later time, but the truth is, once we have taken that side road, we have told ourselves that our goal is not important or not as important as this other issue, and our minds will place less positive emphasis on the goal until the goal becomes a peripheral issue itself, something not really worthy of our attention or energy. Then later on, when the issue that distracted us is resolved, we may not be as "positively charged" about that goal, may even tell ourselves it really wasn't that important to begin with. Later in our lives we may eventually wonder what ever happened to our goal, not realizing that we simply lost our focus.

This may seem a crazy scenario, but it happens more often than many of us realize. I am not saying you should not pay attention to other things happening around you, but that you should not lose focus on what is important to you right now, that goal you have set for yourself, you must keep that in front of you at all times, even if you do get distracted or have to deal with other issues, even while dealing with those issues, keep that goal in focus.

Let me give you an example. Let's say your main goal is to become an accomplished writer, and you see yourself getting closer to that goal every day as you keep focused on that goal, but then tragedy strikes! Let's say a member of your family ends up being diagnosed with a disease or condition that changes everybody's life around him. Of course, you will want to help him or her, you want to be there for them and you may find yourself focusing on them as their happiness or well-being is the most important thing to you at the time.

You can put your writing aside, in this instance, and say to yourself "this is more important, I will focus on him (or her) and get back to my goal later" or you can remain focused on your writing and use this to further your own goal, for instance you can start researching and writing about that condition, you can write about people who have overcome that condition, or you can write about the different ways to combat it, to live with it or to defeat it and crush it. This not only keeps you focused on your goal of writing, but it also goes toward helping that person to deal with what they are going through.

This is just one example, but you see what I am getting at. You may have to be very creative, but you can keep focused on your goal while dealing with other things that may crop up in your life, you MUST keep focused on your goal if you are to achieve it, regardless of what is happening around you. Focus on those things important to you, but keep your goal in front of you while dealing with those other issues, using the issues to further your own goal. You may find that focusing on the goal will help you in dealing with other issues much better than if you took your focus off of your goal and placed your focus entirely on the issue.

Now that we have gotten this peripheral issue out of the way, the main point in this chapter isn't just keeping your mind focused on the goal and not allowing peripheral issues to make you lose your focus or change your focus. The main point of this chapter is also to not allow yourself to focus only on the outcome of your goal. That is to say, don't just focus on where you want to be, focus on where you are and how you are getting there.

Let's go back to the car analogy. Let's say you decide you want to go visit a good friend across town. You know where they live, so navigating to their house is no problem, but what if all you did was kept in your mind where your friend's house was and paid no attention to where you were in relation to his house? What if, instead of looking around you and seeing where you were at, you just started driving toward his or her house with your eyes focused on the distance, to where you want to go? Chances are, you would get lost pretty quickly and would probably never make it to your friend's house.

Obviously when you want to go somewhere, you have to be focused on where you are in relation to where you want to go. You have to notice what street you are on and recognize where the turns are. Not to mention you need to be aware of any road work, obstacles, traffic lights and stop signs, etc. in order to not end up getting in a wreck. In other words, you need to be focused on where you are in order to get to where you want to be.

The same holds true for your goals. When you are focusing on obtaining a goal, you cannot simply focus on the end of the goal, or achieving that goal, but rather you need to focus on the here and now. You need to focus on what you are doing today to reach that goal. Your destination is important, but you will never reach it if you don't focus on where you are going right now. For some reason this is often overlooked by many people. Many people believe that focusing on their goals mean that they have to have this picture of themselves reaching that goal and focus on that picture and if they do this the here and now will take care of itself, but obviously it doesn't work that way. The future is written by the present and if you take your eyes off of where you are in the present, that future will never be written. You can dream of your goal all you want, you can keep envisioning your goal as much as you like, but unless and until you focus on what you are doing RIGHT NOW to obtain that goal, it will always remain a vision and a dream.

Kālidāsa wrote, "Yesterday is only a dream and tomorrow a vision, but today well lived makes every yesterday a dream of happiness and every tomorrow a vision of prosperity." and if you think on this little treasure of wisdom you can see how true it is. The truth is, we have no control over our past, what is past is past. We have no control over our future as it has yet to be written. What we do have control over is today, this moment in time. That is the only thing we can really control, so this is where our focus needs to be if we are to be successful.

The flip side of this is that there also people who tend to live in their past and allow their past to dictate what their future will be. We briefly touched on this earlier in this book, but it is something that bears repeating. When we focus on our past failures, we are only setting ourselves up for failure. One thing you should realize, from the outset, is that you should not see past failures as a defeats. Edison once remarked about his many attempts to invent the lightbulb, "I have not failed. I've just found 10,000 ways that won't work." That's the mindset that most of us should strive to have. If we try something and we don't succeed, we can use that to learn from and the next time we try we will be more equipped for success from our past lesson. We don't dwell on it, saying to ourselves "I can't do it, I tried and failed", but rather "Each attempt I make is bringing me one step closer to success!"

While our past does help in forming who we are becoming, it is not important to dwell on it, as there really is nothing you can do about your past, other than learn from your mistakes. Everybody makes mistakes, it's all part of life, but you must realize that just because you make mistakes that is no reason those mistakes need to make you. Learn from your past, but don't let it consume you, don't let it dictate who you are. You cannot control the past any more than you can control your future. The only real time, as was stated before, is the here and now. You must make the most of the now, and your past will take care of itself, as will your future.

This is why throughout this book I have tried to emphasize that when we make positive affirmations we should always make it in the present tense. We don't say "I am going to accomplish great things" but rather we say "I am accomplishing great things!". We don't say "I will be successful in all my endeavors", but we say "I am successful in all that I am doing". This not only helps us to keep our minds focused on the positive, but also helps us to focus on the here and now. This is the ONLY WAY we can reach our destination, not by focusing on where are going, nor on where we have been, but where we are right now.

BECOMING SELF-AWARE

Everything we have touched on so far in this book hinges on your being aware of your own mind, your own thoughts, how you react to situations and where you are focused. Without being aware of yourself, you cannot achieve any measure of success in changing your attitude or your life. This chapter is dedicated to the principle of actually becoming more aware of who you are, how you think and where you are in relationship to where you want to be.

Let me tell you at the outset, in becoming self-aware there is a danger of slipping into the old pattern of negativity. We may realize that we are weak-minded, that we allow others to guide our choices, that we don't focus on the here and now or a whole host of other things about ourselves that we don't like. The temptation is there to focus on those negative things and say "this is how I am" and in essence allow ourselves to actually strengthen those negative aspects, as our minds says "okay, this is who I am, so this is who I must be".

The trick is not to see the negative in your "self" but the potential positive. Let's say you examine yourself and realize that you are easily led by others, rather than taking control of your own life. You realize this is something that is hindering you and you want to change this about yourself. There is only one way to really change this, and that's by telling your "self" that this is not who you are. It may have been the way you acted in the past, but that was then, this is now. Who you really are is a self-motivated, in charge person. Instead of saying "I am so easily led by others" tell yourself "I am in control! I lead myself. I have complete freedom to make my own choices" and other affirmations. Remember to keep your words positive in every aspect of your affirmations, don't say "I will not be led by others" but rather "I lead myself". And "I am in control of my own decisions".

The whole goal of becoming more aware of your "self" is to become the person you can be, not the person you have convinced yourself you are. If there is anything negative to self, you should examine it, as something you are not, not as something you are. It is all in your mind, and it does not need to be realized as a fact, but rather as something that is keeping you from becoming who you are meant to be. The more you examine the self, the more potential you have for changing your attitude to becoming more positive minded. You do not need to be scared of who you find locked within your mind, you should be ecstatic to find that there is some little voice in your head telling you "I am shy and intimidated around people", because once you have exposed this lie, you can tell that voice to shut up, you can tell yourself "I am confident about myself and people love me", and believe it to be true, because it is true.

I once had a great friend who was very smart and very enjoyable to be around, but he had one quirk that almost drove me crazy. If asked for his opinion, he invariably gave you your own opinion back to you. Let me clarify this, let's say I were to ask him, "What do you think about raising the minimum wage? Would it be good or bad for the economy?" he would immediately ask me what i thought (if I hadn't already made my own opinion clear on this) and then he would simply agree. I have to admit, there were many who didn't even seem to notice this habit of his, but it drove me crazy, until one day I finally asked him why he never really had an opinion on anything, but always just agreed with the majority or agreed with the other person.

Of course, he agreed with me that this was something he did! But, he said he had no idea why he did that, or even realized he was doing it. Once I pointed it out to him that this was, indeed, what he did time and again, it made him more aware of this habit. As we talked about it, we came to realize that he was simply avoiding hurting someone else's feelings. He realized that people wanted him to agree with him, so he agreed with them, regardless of his own personal convictions. Once he became aware of this tendency in himself, he realized that he really could disagree, in most cases, without anyone becoming angry or hurt. While it is true that some people cannot stand to have others disagree with them, for the most part people are more than willing to listen to and discuss alternative or opposing views. It is how we learn and grow.

After my friend became aware of this, he started working on it. He decided that, instead of just agreeing with others, he would offer his opinion, even if it was contrary to the other person's opinion. He realized that he was an agreeable sort, so taking this step may be uncomfortable, but he was willing to take that step, especially after realizing that his agreeability was often dishonest, which was a trait he did not like to see in himself. After a few months, I noticed a marked improvement in his conversing skills as did others. While many did not really know what the change was, they could tell there was more depth in their conversations with him. He finally told me, years later, that by helping him realize this in himself, I literally changed his life. He became more confident in other aspects of his life, he stopped worrying about saying something offensive, though he was still conscientious of others feelings. One day his wife told me, the one trait that really drew her to him, that made her fall in love with him was that he wasn't afraid to speak his mind.

In order to set about becoming self-aware, you must examine the way you react to those things around you. Your actions, or your reactions, are based on your own self-image. How do you react when someone gives you a compliment? Do you accept the compliment and thank that person, do you become anxious or uncomfortable and mumble a quick thank you? Do you actually argue or discount the compliment? There are a number of ways we might react to a compliment and each of these ways reveals something about who we are. If you can graciously accept a compliment without modesty, without shyness, without hesitation than this shows self-confident person. If you feel uncomfortable when given a compliment, you may have some problems accepting yourself as being that person others might see in you. If you completely deny a compliment, then you definitely have a problem with believing in yourself.

So one of the first things you should examine is how DO you react to a compliment. Be honest with yourself. Does it make you feel uncomfortable? Why? Do you think yourself unworthy? If so, why? Don't be afraid to examine yourself and your reaction closely, as by doing so you may discover one of those "voices" we spoke of a couple paragraphs back.

For example, at one point in my life, I can say I was a fairly shy person. When someone would compliment me, for instance saying "wow! you are very smart!" I would tell myself "this person doesn't really know me, if they found out how dumb I was, they wouldn't like me". Of course, I didn't realize it at the time that there was this voice saying that in my head, but I do remember feeling almost afraid of the compliment. I would either pretend not to have heard the compliment, so I wouldn't be obligated to acknowledge the compliment, or I would stammer out something like "no not really" so as not to raise the person's expectations of who I really was (or who I thought I was).

It wasn't until years later, when I discovered the power in positive thinking and realized how to become self-aware that I became aware of this tendency in my own self. I then realized that what that person was saying was true, but the voices in my head were the false ones. I could accept that compliment and thank that person, first for recognizing the quality in me and second for helping me to recognize that quality in myself. I could say, confidently, "Thank you so much! That's very kind of you to say so.". Of course, now I can accept compliments and I actually like compliments as they go right along with my own positive affirmations, it's always nice to have someone echo your own positive affirmations, but also when you become a more positive minded person, you will find that people WILL compliment you much more as they recognize that you are a positive force in this world and you are a great person!

One of the greatest moments in my own life was that moment that I realized that I could not only accept a compliment but take pride in that compliment and let others know how happy I am that they realized that person within me. The reaction that I saw from others to my reaction was amazing, they became even friendlier, they actually liked me more when I accepted their compliment as a genuine affirmation of some quality I possessed. In short, I became more confident, they became more interested in me and we became friends. But first, before I was able to achieve this level of confidence, I had to understand why I reacted the way I did, then I had to get rid of that voice telling me I wasn't worthy of such praise. I had to start telling myself, I am worthy of praise and adulation, I really am smart, I am really a great person.

It may seem very hard to contradict that voice at first. It may almost seem as if you are lying to yourself, but once you begin doing this, you will soon realize that the positive affirmation isn't the lie, it was that voice in the first place that is the lie. You really are a great person, but that voice within you is telling you that you aren't. If you can realize, as you practice positive thinking and affirmations, that you are finally being HONEST with yourself, then you will find it much easier to overcome those negative thoughts that previously kept you from being who you truly are and realizing the awesome potential within yourself to be who you have always wanted to be.

This is only one reaction you will want to examine in order to become more self-aware. In truth, you should examine every reaction you can find. How you react to sad news, how you react to adversity, how you react in social situations, how you react to change, etc. All of these reactions will give you a chance to examine the reason behind the reaction, what is that voice telling you when you react to this situation. If you react to sad news by denying it or deflecting it, is it because it frightens you? Is that voice telling you, "This is because of something you did" (even when you know it is not) or is that voice, perhaps telling you that "if it happened to such and such, it will surely happen to you!"... regardless of what the voice is telling you, find the negative aspects of that voice and then replace them with positive "I am in control of my life" is a great generic affirmation when that voice tries to tell you that something is out of your control, or something is your fault when you had nothing to do with it. It is an affirmation that YOU are Responsible for YOU and not things that have nothing to do with you, but it is affirming it in a positive manner.

I believe this is one thing many people really have a lot of problem with. The realization that they are responsible for themselves and their own actions, and not other people's actions. There are many people who feel they need to be in control, not only of themselves but in everybody and everything around them. These are the people who react to other people in hostile or negative ways when they act or say something that is unexpected or in opposition to their own beliefs. It is as though they believe that they are responsible for the other person believing as they do, and if the other person is in disagreement then they take this as a personal affront, as some sort of personal failure. I'm sure everybody know someone like this, but if you don't then you might take a look at yourself because you may be that type of person. If you react to any opposition of your own belief or opinion with anger and hostility, then you need to realize this reaction is not really going to help you grow, to become a positive minded person, to learn new and different ways of looking at life or to being an enjoyable person to know and to hang around.

There is one other reaction that you need to look at, and this reaction is so important that we are going to cover it in detail in the next chapter. This is how you react to negativity in others. This is a big one, because often we find ourselves becoming negative around negativity, almost as if someone else's negativity rubs off on us. As we have said in a previous chapter, the power of negativity is a very strong force, and this not only in ourselves, but in others as well to negatively charge us. We can overcome this negativity however in much the same way we have overcome our own negativity, by positive thinking and positive affirmations.

OVERCOMING NEGATIVITY IN OTHERS

I remember not too long ago meeting someone who I really cared a lot about. This person had some great qualities and was really a very wonderful person, but one of the "bad" things about them is that they were negative minded. They tended to always react to situations by making negative affirmations. For instance, when we got low on money they would tell me, "we aren't going to be able to pay our bills!" or "we're never going to get ahead" or something along those lines. Having overcome my own negativity I immediately saw this in them, and tried to help them, but they would insist that they were not being negative, they would say they were just being real.

I can remember the arguments that often ensued by my trying to get them to see their negativity,.To be honest, I became depressed and started finding myself slipping back into negativity, almost as if their negativity was a contagious disease and my positive immune system was being wore down. It was at this point that I realized, those voices that I had to overcome within myself came not only from my own mind, but were actually based in what others said to me.

The feeling of uselessness came from my father confirming how useless I was when I was young. My father was a good man and he loved his children, but he didn't realize how his words could affect us, and often his words were very negative. I had teachers and students telling me I was dumb in school, even though I knew I wasn't, but I ended up believing it and affirming it. I could go on for a whole chapter describing the different negative affirmations I was fed as I grew up, and i grew to accept them and then to reaffirm them to myself until I believed them.

To be honest, it wasn't until I met this special person that I realized that this was the main source of my prior negativity, as I began to hear those negative voices again in my head telling me how useless it was to try, how things are never going to get better, that life is unfair and we can't be what we want to be. Even though I am now (and was at the time I met this person) a very positive minded individual, making my daily positive affirmations and very confident in myself, the negativity was still there and I was still affected by that negativity. I realized, through my own self examination that the negative voices I thought were dead were actually coming back to life and I realized those voices were echoing that voice of the one I cared very much about.

Had it not been my practice of examining every reaction I have, I may have not even understood the source of my own negativity or realized I was becoming a negative person again, but thankfully I recognized that the reason I was becoming depressed and negative was because I was actually accepting someone else's negativity. Instead of reacting to that negativity as I would the negative voices within myself, I reacted to it as if it were a matter of truth and I accepted it at face value. Even after this realization it took me quite a while to figure out how to deal with that person's negativity.

I didn't want to distance myself from them (which would be one viable solution, to remove yourself from the negativity) as I cared very deeply for them and wanted them in my life. I tried arguing with them and explaining their negativity, but (as I've said) they would deny that it was negativity and state that they were just being real. I told myself daily that I am a positive person and I am overcoming all negativity within and without, which actually did help quite a bit, but I still had to deal with their negativity.

Then I hit upon the only way I could combat their negativity without getting into an argument. I started countering the negativity with positive affirmations as if I was making my own positive affirmations. For instance, when this person would say "we are never going to get ahead" I would say "we can get ahead if we do such and such". If they were to say, "We aren't even going to be able to pay our bills" I would say "We will have to buckle down, we can pay our bills if we do such and such". In essence I would not actually say they were wrong, I would just take the negative and affirmation and turn it around into a positive affirmation. That person I am speaking of, we are still together and they have become more and more positive as the years go on. To be sure, they still have negativity, but it's becoming less of a problem and they are even learning to overcome it by realizing the power in positive affirmations and positive thinking.

I've brought up this real life instance to make a point. The only true way to overcome a negative is by using a positive. If you hear a voice of negativity saying "we can't" or "you can't" turn it into a "We can" or "I can", not in an argumentative way, but rather in a way to allow both yourself and that person see that there is indeed a solution. You might have to take some sort of action for it to become a reality, but to say something can't be done is to allow yourself to be defeated, and we are not defeatist we are overcomers! There is nothing you cannot do, no goal you cannot reach, if you affirm the positive and allow yourself to realize the potential within yourself as well as others. Do not be overcome by negative, but overcome negative through positive.

You should also be aware that not only friends, family and acquaintances might be spreading negative affirmations around, but often the news, television shows, movies, the newspaper, books, the internet and a whole plethora of other sources are also capable of spreading negativity. By becoming aware of these sources of negativity and becoming aware of the "cant's" and "won'ts" and such as you read, hear or watch them, you can still use positive affirmations.

When you hear something like "You can't seem to break free of your debt" (which is actually from a commercial for debt consolidation) you should recognize that negativity and reinforce within your mind (and possibly make a vocal affirmation as well) "I am in control of my debt" or "I am able to do whatever i need to do to be happy" or something along those lines. Whatever your affirmation is, it should be personal and believable to you. You will find that, after a while, it's an automatic defence mechanism when you hear negativity, the shield of positive thinking goes up, the sword of positive reaffirmations goes up and you are able time and again to overcome any and all negativity, whether it is within you or outside of you, you have control and you will always be the victor over negativity.

On the other hand, if you do find a certain program on television is so negative that you find yourself having to put on this shield over and over again, and do battle with negativity than it might be a good idea to find something better on, or if there is a "friend" on facebook who only seems to post negative things and you find it's becoming a bother to read and reaffirm the positive 20 times a day, then unfriend them or block their posts. If it's a person in your life that seems to always be bringing negativity into your life, you might evaluate how much you value their friendship and whether it might simply be a better idea to distance yourself from that friend. As the old saying goes, "choose your battles", sometimes you might need to battle that negativity, but often your best course of action is to simply walk away.

OVERCOMING PROCRASTINATION

One of the best ways to avoid success in life is by procrastinating. Many people are plagued by this ongoing condition that hampers them in so many aspects of their lives, some are chronic procrastinators while others only procrastinate doing those things that may cause them to be uncomfortable or that takes them out of their comfort zone. Either way, procrastinations is a sure-fire way to sabotage yourself and your chance at succeeding in life.

By procrastinating you are actually placing obstacles in your own path, you are keeping yourself from seeing yourself as a success. When you put things off you tend to feel defeated, if only unconsciously. You might as well be telling yourself, "I can't do it" when you tell yourself "I'll do it later". You are basically making an excuse to avoid doing something that you need to do, and even things you want to do. Chronic procrastination evolved from years and years of practicing this self-defeating mental attitude. At first you may have learned to procrastinate when you were just a child, and you may have even developed this habit as a form of rebellion. For instance when your father told you to clean your room, you may have said "I will do it later".

If you take the time, however, to look back at all the times you have procrastinated, you will more than likely realize that in almost every case, the outcome was not good. It may seem "safer" to put things off, or it may seem easier to put them off, but in reality putting things off is detrimental to our success in life and especially in our ability to maintain a positive outlook on our own life and our own abilities.

For many people procrastination becomes a lifestyle cutting across all aspects of their life. They are late in paying bills and late for appointments (or they miss them altogether), they wait till the very last minute to do their holiday shopping, they tend to be late in filing their income taxes... the list goes on. Many people who are chronic procrastinators never really even realize this aspect of their self. Those who do see this in themselves may often feel powerless to change this about themselves. However, as we have already learned if we have been paying attention to this book, this can be overcome through positive affirmations and self-examination.

As a matter of fact, just recognizing this aspect of your personality is over half the battle. Once you realize that you were a procrastinator, you can take steps to change this. Notice, that I said "were a procrastinator". That's the way you should be thinking, when you notice something in your nature that has kept you from succeeding. You should avoid saying "I AM a procrastinator!" but instead recognize that this was who you were, not who you are (or desire to be). Once you realize that this was what you were, you can decide that you will be a person of decisive action. You can make the positive affirmation that "I will do what needs to be done when it needs to be done" or you can put it in your own words that have the most meaning to you, but be sure to keep it positive.

The best way, however, to overcome this self-defeating activity of procrastination is to realize that there is no "later", there is only now. We learned this already from the previous chapters, but we need to recognize this and make it part of our mindset. Just as when we find ourselves saying "can't" we change it to can; when we find ourselves saying "later' we should invariably change this to "now", if it's at all possible. If it can be done now, then we should do it now. If it's something that's very important, like paying our bills or calling on a sick relative, by putting it off we may seriously regret our decision later. Once we have gotten in the habit of living in the now, it becomes much more difficult for us to procrastinate. If we know we need to do something, and we have the means to accomplish it, we don't think "later', because in our minds there is no later, in reality there is no later, there is only now.

I cannot emphasize strongly enough how important it is to not put things off, unless you cannot do them in the present (for instance, if you need to save your money up, or it's a goal that requires small steps to achieving). You should take each moment as it comes and live it to the fullest, doing what needs to be done while there is time to do it. Once you start overcoming procrastination and you realize how much it has held you back, you will find it easier and easier to live in the here and now, to complete what you need to do and you will begin to realize that by not procrastinating you have managed to reduce your stress level significantly while at the same time increasing your positive attitude.

NO TIME LIKE THE PRESENT

As we have discussed throughout this book, when making positive affirmations and working on positive thought patterns, you don't focus on the future by saying "I will be more successful" or whatever affirmation you are making, you say "I am more successful" or "I am a successful person". The future is not yet written, the past only a memory, the only real time is NOW. You might set your goals in the future, but you work on meeting those goals in the present, in every moment you focus on the present and in seeing that you are doing your best to meet your goals.

In a previous chapters we touched on this idea of focusing on the present, but this is such an important subject I feel we need to close this book by reaffirming that in order to change your life, you must start now, you should have already begun this process of changing your mind to be more positive. If you haven't affirmed this, do it now, tell yourself "I am changing my life now" and "I am a positive person", say it and believe it because as you believe it you will achieve it. Don't just try to do it, do it or don't do it, there is no try (in the words of Yoda). When you tell yourself "I will try to become more positive" you are not making a positive affirmation, you are telling yourself "I am not positive", at least that's what your unconscious mind is hearing and realizing.

When you say "I am more positive" your subconscious mind may at first be jolted by this revelation, but as you continue to affirm it, believe it or not (on the other hand, just believe it, and leave out the not) you will find it to be true. Your subconscious mind will begin to "realize" it, that is it will make it real. Your reality is what you convince yourself to be real, as well as what you allow others to convince you to be real. Don't forget that, because that realization in and of itself can change your entire life, when you accept it.

So, don't say to yourself, this has been an interesting book, I'm going to start trying to practice these principles soon and see how they work. That was then, that was the old you, this is now, this is the real you and the real you knows that "later" is a figment of your imagination, you can do nothing later, you can only do it now! So stop living in the past or in the future, but start living in the the here and now. You have the power within yourself to start living the life you were meant to live, free of doubts and fears, free of reservations and negative thoughts. But if you decide to put it off, you have made a decision to not go for that dream. Later may never come. Tomorrow is not guaranteed. The present is the only time you have and if you don't take advantage of the present you will find that your opportunity may have slipped away.

Within the pages of this short book is a secret that has propelled more people to success than any single principle, any single thought or philosophy.in the history of mankind. Seems like a lofty claim, I am sure, but if you go through any kind of philosophy that promises you success, or if you examine any successful person to find out how they achieved that success, you will find this underlying principle of positive thinking. You will find that success is almost entirely based on your own belief in your own abilities regardless of any other outside influence. You will also find that those people who have become successful realized that the concept of the future is not a reality, but belongs to the dreamer. You can surely dream of the future you can even hope for the future, but if you try to live in the future, you will find that it's just not real.

On the other side of that coin, your past is a memory, it is not real time. You may have failed at something in the past, but that was then. You may have tried to do something and found you couldn't do it, and you may think that because you couldn't do it then, you can't do it now. That's a lie and you had better get that lie out of your head (you know how, don't you?) because that lie will hold you back and keep you from realizing the potential you have in the here and now. If you are living in the past, you are living in a memory, you aren't experiencing the awesome gift of the present, and you aren't realizing the potential you have within yourself. The only time you should be focusing on is the here and now, because this is the only time you have, the rest is all in your mind, the past is a dream and tomorrow a vision, but today is real.

Now, please don't get it twisted and think that I am saying you should not plan for your future or that you shouldn't have any goals for your future. Planning is an essential part of life and you most certainly should examine what you can do to have success in the future. For instance, you wouldn't purchase a new house or a new car without first sitting down and examining your budget to see if you can afford the future payments on that house or car or boat or whatever. I am not at all advocating that you simply ignore the future, but I am saying the only way you can ensure a good future is by living in the present. You will never reach your future goals if you are not living in the here and now. It's what you do today that makes tomorrow a success or a failure. It is what you do NOW that determines what you will be doing tomorrow.

Procrastination can be a real enemy. Many people put off doing what they feel may be hard or uncomfortable. However, you must realize that by putting something off that needs to be done, you are only adding unnecessary stress and often you are denying yourself the joy of overcoming an obstacle. If there is something that really needs to be done, then you must do it. Not tomorrow, not in a few minutes, if you have the opportunity to do it now, than you need to do it now. Procrastination is just another tool of negativity, it is that voice inside your head saying "you can't do this, at least not right now" and it's a reaction that you need to observe in yourself and then rid yourself of. You need to tell yourself "I am a man (or woman) of action! I will do it NOW!"

So what are you going to do when you finish reading this book? Are you going to sigh and say, well that would be nice, and then go about your previous existence hoping that maybe tomorrow you can find the ability to start practicing the power of positive thinking? Are you going to finish reading this book and sigh and say, if only this was true, but my past shows me to be such and such? Or are you going to finish reading this book and start living your life as the person you are meant to be, unafraid of the past, unconcerned for the future, knowing that as you live each moment with the knowledge that all things are possible to those who believe that you will achieve your highest potential and do what you have always wanted to do.

The choice is yours to make. I do hope you realize that every word you have read is true, that there are no platitudes within these pages. I have not been feeding you a pipe dream here, in hopes that you might be lucky and realize your potential. I have been giving you the secret to overcoming your own limitations, but I can't overcome them for you. You have to start believing, you have to start affirming. And you have to start right now.

So, let me just close this book by congratulating you on the new life you have started. I am very happy to know that you will now be free from those bonds that bound you to a dreary life of wishing and hoping but never achieving. I am so happy to know that you are now on a new journey, one that promises that anything you can dream you can achieve. Congratulations, as today truly is the first day of the rest of your life.

Printed in Great Britain
by Amazon